# Multi-Cooker Cookbook for Beginners

Instant Weight Loss Cookbook. Cooking Your Way To A Healthy Weight With, For Anyone Who Loves Effortless Tasty Food On A Tight Budget with Air Fryer and Slow Cooker.

# Table of Contents

Additionally, the information in the following pages is intended only for informational purposes and should thus be thought of as universal. As befitting its nature, it is presented without assurance regarding its prolonged validity or interim quality. Trademarks that are mentioned are done without written consent and can in no way be considered an endorsement from the trademark holder.

# INTRODUCTION

Cooking for beginners appears like a painless enough task; however, when you begin to cook, you must take many different criteria into mind. First, it is pretty essential to be secure in your kitchen. Take plenty of time to take a look over your kitchen, you may not know your way around it, to begin with, but soon enough you will be at ease sufficient to gather new abilities and create things off of your new-found know-how. The second thing you want to do is to recognize some standard terms.

Cooking terms help you to understand your way through recipes and cookbooks. As you begin, you will often see terminology like sauté, brown or mince, and chop. It is beneficial to know these terms when getting started; that is why you will need to be familiar with cooking conditions and the vocabulary of cooking before you get going. After learning the terms, it will be much easier to go along with a recipe correctly. As you read through a recipe and see something, you don't know to take a moment to look the word up. Examine the recipe first to help make sure that you have got all the ingredients, and you are comfortable with the terms.

You should not set out to cook a recipe without finding all the items and knowing what you are going to do with them. This is understood as mise en place, French for everything in its place. There is nothing at all worse than getting started down the road with a recipe and finding out that you need a key part. You should also make sure that you have an operating understanding of utensils and the type of utensils you will need to finish the recipe. For instance, if you are proceeding to make muffins, you would possibly need to have that muffin pan! Once you acquaint yourself with the equipment and lingo of the trade, you will be on your way to pursuing recipes and cooking food in no time.

As with anything else, practice makes perfect.

There is a lot of learning that must be done to become a good cook, and then there is becoming a great cook. But that takes time and plenty of dishes that could have come out better - and they will-someday. But that's O.K.

Everyone starts somewhere. And the best place to start cooking for beginners is in the kitchen, of course. Naturally, there is all kinds of cooking: American, Chinese, Japanese, Indian, European, etc. All of these types of cooking takes time and training to learn how to master the basics. But it can be done because it has been by many already. Maybe you are not the best cook yet, and perhaps that may never happen. But always remember that someone is not quite as good as you. Probably you'll be better than most ever will be. O.K. so much for having the right attitude and self-esteem. Whatever your reason for cooking or learning to cook, you should always begin with the basics. The first thing that you need to learn is what the different terminology you will find in recipes means. There are many new and sometimes foreign sounding terms that you will find in familiar recipes. These terms can mean the difference in recipe success or failure. You should be able to see the right section in any comprehensive cookbook that explains the different definitions for unfamiliar terminology. If you aren't sure what is meant by "folding in the eggs," it is in your best interest to look it up.

So take this valuable hint: Try simple recipes at first and then get a little braver by tackling a few more difficult dishes. Many recipes will tell you just how difficult it is to make. But you will soon know by just looking at the recipe. Another good idea is that once you get some experience with different (successful) dishes, make yourself a catalog or diary of dishes that went over well. Put the date and comments in the diary. This will come in handy when you don't know what to cook or a special occasion is coming, and you want to be sure to make it successful and fun.

As you learn new recipes and improve your culinary skills and talents you will discover that preparing your meals from scratch is much more rewarding than preparing prepackaged meals that are purchased from the shelves of your local supermarkets. You will also find as your experience and confidence grows that you will find yourself more and more often improvising as you go and adjusting recipes to meet your personal preferences.

So what's the secret to learning the basics and becoming a good

# YOGURT SMASH!

There are so many types of yogurt in the grocery store: some low in fat and high in sugar, some with cute animal pictures. Some are Greek. Some have chocolate shavings and candy. Some have names like "key lime pie."

Now forget about all of that. The best value for your money is the big buckets of plain yogurt. The fat content is your choice—just check that it doesn't contain gelatin, and you're all set. Starting with plain yogurt, you can make super flavors in your own kitchen, where you know exactly what's going into it.

If you have kids, ask them what flavors they can imagine and make it! It's a lot more fun than letting the supermarket choose for you.

If you want a thicker Greek-style yogurt, all you have to do is a strain regular American yogurt through cheesecloth to remove the extra water.

Yogurt's versatility makes it a great staple to keep in the fridge. Mix it with some of the items you see on the next page or turn it into a savory sauce like raita or tzatziki.

# CHAPTER 3: LUNCH

Preparing lunch for the whole family is not very easy, especially if you want to please everyone's palate. Add to the that the hectic accidents that happen in the morning as everyone gets ready for school and work, and you know that the only way to start the day right is to make sure that you stick to easy recipes that would provide everyone a satisfying but healthy lunch.

Anything complex will probably mean late kids or asking them to eat cafeteria food. Take-out lunches should be forgotten because there are so many healthy lunch solutions that can easily be taken to the office, to school, and anywhere else you may need to go. Listed below are some tasty recipes which include delicious fresh produce such as fresh vegetables and lean protein, which will fuel you for the rest of the day so that your body will not feel deprived.

# AVOCADO SALAD BAGEL

A great addition to a lunchbox.
This is a tasty and colorful addition to any lunchbox and is ideal for taking to school or work. So simple to make and also a great way of getting 2 of your 5-a-day.

## Ingredients - Serves 1 Adult

- ½ a wholemeal bagel, toasted

- 1 tablespoon of frozen sweetcorn

- ¼ an avocado, chopped or mashed

- Pinch of paprika

- Pinch of chili powder (optional)

- 2 lettuce leaves

- 4 slices of tomato

- 1 slice of onion

- 4 slices of cucumber

## Method

1. Quickly defrost the sweetcorn by microwaving it for approximately 15 seconds.

2. Toast your bagel, and as it is toasting, combine the avocado with the defrosted sweetcorn, paprika, and chili powder.

3. Place the lettuce leaves, tomato, onion, and cucumber slices on the toasted bagel and top with the avocado mixture.

## Serving Suggestions

Want some extra protein? Add flaked tuna to the avocado mixture.

## Info

Use seeded bagels to increase your intake of good dietary fats.

# AVOCADO SALAD SANDWICH

Suitable for vegetarians

This fresh sandwich is easy to prepare, and the combination of the whole grain bread and fresh vegetables gives it a real crunch.

## Ingredients - Serves 1 Adult

- 2 slices of wholegrain bread

- 1 teaspoon of wholegrain mustard

- 2 leaves of lettuce

- 4 slices of cucumber

- 2 slices of ripe tomato

- ¼ of a ripe avocado, sliced into strips

- 55g / 2 oz. of grated carrot

## Method

1. Spread the mustard onto each side of the bread

2. Place the lettuce leaves and tomato slices and any other optional ingredients on one side of the bread

3. Top the whole thing with the remaining slice of bread

4. Wrap up in cling film and store in your lunchbox

## Serving Suggestions

To keep your lunches interesting each day, swap the mustard for tomato relish, spicy mango chutney, or even cool mint-infused natural yogurt!

# BACON AND SWEETCORN BAKED POTATO

A tasty alternative to sandwiches for lunch.

Baked potatoes are versatile, and you can add your favorite filling.

## Ingredients - Serves 2 Adults

- 2 large potatoes scrubbed but not peeled

- 4 rashers, with fat trimmed off

- 6 dessertspoons tinned sweetcorn

- Salt and pepper to taste

## Method
1. Preheat the oven to 220°C / 425°F / Gas Mark 7.

2. Wash the potatoes and then prick them all over with a fork.

3. Bake in a pre-heated oven for 1½ hours or until the inside is tender.

4. For the microwave method, follow the instructions given in the manual.

5. Grill the rashers and cut into small pieces.

6. Cut the potato in half and carefully scoop the center out of the potato.

7. Mix this potato with the sweet corn, rashers, and pepper.

8. Return the mixture to potato skin.

9. Place in a hot oven and bake until warmed through and golden.

**Serving Suggestions**

Serve with a side salad of lettuce, tomatoes, red onion, grated carrot, low-fat salad dressing.

# BACON AND TUNA BAKED POTATO

Add your favorite filling.

This is a tasty alternative to sandwiches for lunch. Baked potatoes are versatile, and you can add your favorite filling.

### Ingredients - Serves 2 Adults

- 2 large potatoes, scrubbed but not peeled

- 200g / 7 oz. can of tuna fish

- 100g / 4 oz. Back bacon, fat trimmed off, approx. 4 rashers

- Salt and pepper to taste

### Method
1. Preheat the oven to 220°C / 425°F/ Gas Mark 7.

2. Wash the potatoes, then prick them all over with a fork.

3. Bake in a pre-heated oven for 1½ hours or until the inside is tender.

4. For the microwave method, follow the instructions given in the manual.

5. Grill the bacon until crisp then crumble into small pieces.

6. Cut the potato in half and carefully scoop out the center of the potato.

7. Mix the potato with the tuna and bacon.

8. Return the mixture to the potato skins.

9. Place in a hot oven and bake until warmed through and slightly browned on top.

## Serving Suggestions

Serve with a side salad- lettuce, tomatoes, red onion, grated carrot, low-fat salad dressing

# BAGEL WITH TURKEY AND AVOCADO

Quick and Easy

Are you thinking of a way to use up leftover turkey? Look no further we have the perfect lunch recipe for you!

## Ingredients - Serves 1 Adult

- ½ a wholemeal bagel, toasted

- ¼ of an avocado

- 2 slices of turkey

- 4 slices of tomato

- 4 slices of cucumber

- 2 lettuce leaves

## Method

Top the toasted bagel with the other ingredients to keep hunger at bay until your next meal.

## Serving Suggestions

Serve with a side salad.

## Info

Why not give poppy seed, sesame seed, or multiseed bagels a go?

## About this Recipe

A healthy lunch option is providing nutrients such as fiber, protein, and vitamin C.

# BANG BANG CHICKEN SALAD

Tasty and Nutritious

In need of some salad inspiration? We've got the answer right here! This oriental recipe will be a crowd-pleaser, and the chili and ginger give it a real kick.

## Ingredients - Serves 1 Adult

For the salad:

- 1 small chicken breast (100g / 3½oz.), sliced horizontally to create 2 thin fillets.

- 1cm / ½" piece of fresh ginger, peeled and grated.

- ¼ red chili, deseeded and thinly sliced.

- 1 teaspoon of vegetable oil.
- 60g / 2oz. of dried rice noodles.

- 150ml / 5fl oz. of boiling water.

- 1 small carrot, peeled and grated or thinly sliced.

- 50g / 2oz. of cucumber, thinly sliced into matchsticks.

- 1 scallion, finely sliced.

- 1 tablespoon of fresh coriander, chopped.

- 1 teaspoon of dry roasted peanuts, crushed.

For the dressing:

- 1 tablespoon of smooth peanut butter.

- 1 tablespoon of water.

- 1 teaspoon of sweet chili sauce.

- ½ lime, juiced.

- 1 teaspoon of reduced-salt soy sauce

**Method**

1. Heat the oil in a nonstick pan, and when hot, add the chicken breast, ginger, and half the fresh chili.

2. Cook for 8–10 minutes, until the chicken is cooked through, turning once. Set aside to cool slightly.

3. Cook the noodles according to packet instructions, and when cooked, drain well.

4. Make the dressing by combining the peanut butter with water, lime juice, sweet chili, and soy sauce.

5. Chop the remainder of the fresh chili as finely as you can and add this to your peanut sauce.

6. When the chicken has cooled slightly, shred or slice it finely and combine with the cooked noodles and coat in the dressing.

7. Once completely cold, add the prepared vegetables, stirring to coat in the peanut dressing.

8. Before serving, scatter with the freshly chopped coriander and crushed dry roasted peanuts.

## Serving Suggestions

Serve with a slice of lime on the side.

## Info

If you're feeling adventurous, why not add a little more chili to give this recipe an extra kick!

## About this Recipe

This colorful recipe is a  great way of introducing new flavors such as ginger and coriander into your child's diet.

# BEANS AND CHEESE BAKED A POTATO

Baked potatoes are versatile.

This is a tasty alternative to sandwiches for lunch. Baked potatoes are versatile, and you can add your favorite filling.

### Ingredients - Serves 2 Adults

- 2 large potatoes, scrubbed but not peeled.

- 1 x 225g / 8 oz. small can of baked beans.

- 55g / 2 oz. of low-fat cheddar cheese, grated.

- Salt and pepper to taste.

### Method

1. Preheat the oven to 220°C / 425°F / Gas Mark 7.

2. Wash the potatoes and then prick them all over with a fork.

3. Bake in a pre-heated oven for 1½ hours or until the inside is tender.

4. For the microwave method, follow the instructions given in the manual.
5. Heat the baked beans in a saucepan on the hob or in the microwave according to instructions on the tin.

6. Cut the potato in half and carefully scoop the center out of the potato.

7. Mix this potato with the baked beans and pepper.

8. Return the mixture to potato skin and sprinkle with grated cheese.

9. Place in a hot oven and bake until warmed through and golden.

## Serving Suggestions

Serve with a side salad of lettuce, tomatoes, red onion, grated carrot, low-fat salad dressing

# BLT PASTA SALAD

Packed with flavor.

A delicious salad that is ready in only 20 minutes! A great idea for a quick lunch.

### Ingredients - Serves 1 Adult

- 75g of pasta.

- 2 cooked bacon rashers, sliced.

- 45g of spinach, chopped.

- 8 cherry tomatoes, halved.

- ½ tablespoon of crème Fraiche.

- ¼ teaspoon of wholegrain mustard.

## Method

1. Cook pasta according to packet instructions.

2. Mix the bacon, spinach, tomatoes, crème Fraiche and mustard in a bowl along with the pasta and mix well.

## Info

Use low-fat crème Fraiche.

# CAJUN CHICKEN WRAP

Add a spicy kick to your lunchtime!

If you like a spicier filling, add a pinch of chili or a dash of tabasco to the tomato mixture for an extra Cajun kick!

**Ingredients - Serves 1 Adult**

For the wrap:

- 1 wholemeal tortilla wrap.

- 2 tablespoons Cajun seasoning.

- 1 teaspoon paprika.

- 1 grilled chicken breast, sliced.

- 1 teaspoon vegetable oil.

- 1 teaspoon low-fat mayonnaise.

- ½ teaspoon lemon juice.

- 1 spring onion, chopped.

- 4 lettuce leaves.

- 1 fresh basil leaf.

For after:

- 2 small satsumas

## Method
1. Combine all of the ingredients for the wrap in a bowl. Spread the mixture onto your wrap and enjoy warm or cold.

2. Finish off with tangy satsumas or similar-sized fruit such as plums.

## Serving Suggestions

For a spicier taste, why not add some fresh chili pepper?

# CAPRESE PITTA POCKET

Suitable for vegetarians.

Try something different at lunchtime with this Caprese pitta pocket recipe! With this lunch option, you will be well on your way to reaching 5-a-day. Vegetables are a great source of vitamins, minerals, and fiber.

### Ingredients - Serves 1 Adult

For the pitta:

- 1 teaspoon of balsamic vinegar.

- 1 teaspoon of olive oil.

- 3 cherry tomatoes, sliced.

- 30g / 1oz. of low-fat mozzarella cubes.

- 4 slices of cucumber.

- 2 handfuls of fresh spinach (80g / 3oz.)

- 1 scallion, sliced.

- 1 dessertspoon of fresh basil, chopped.

- 4 small lettuce leaves.

- 1 pitta pocket (75g / 2½oz.)

- Black pepper, to taste.

**Method**

1. Mix the balsamic vinegar and oil in a bowl with a fork.

2. Combine all of the other ingredients (except the pitta bread) and mix gently in the bowl.

3. Season with black pepper to taste.

4. Carefully slice open your pitta and fill with the Caprese mix.

**Serving Suggestions**

Choose a wholegrain pitta pocket as an even healthier option.

## Info

Sometimes it is easier to heat your pitta for 30 seconds in the microwave before slicing open.

## About this Recipe

Enjoy your pitta hot or cold. Use a sandwich toaster or place your pitta under a heated grill for 3-4 minutes until the mozzarella is melted.

# CARAMELIZED ONION, MUSHROOM AND CHEESE qUICHE

Suitable for vegetarians.

A tasty variation on the usual quiche recipe, this lower fat version is a filling dish suitable for family meals.

## Ingredients - Serves 8 Adults

For the pastry:

- 120g / 4 oz. of rolled oats.

- 65g / 2½ oz. of plain flour.

- ¼ teaspoon of salt.

- 3 tablespoons of cold, unsalted butter, cut into small pieces.

- 3 tablespoons of cold, low-fat buttermilk.

For the filling:

- 4 teaspoons of olive oil.

- 1 large onion, sliced thinly into half-moons.

- 225g / 8 oz. of sliced mushrooms, try a mixture of edible varieties

- ½ teaspoon salt.

- ¼ teaspoon freshly ground black pepper, to taste.

- ¼ teaspoon dry mustard.

- 1 tablespoon of chopped fresh thyme leaves or 1 teaspoon of dried thyme.

- 6 medium eggs. 3 whole and 3 just whites.

- 255g / 9 oz. of evaporated fat-free milk, not condensed milk.

- 75g / 2½ oz. of low-fat cheddar cheese, grated.

## Method

For the pastry:

1. Preheat the oven to 200°C / 400°F / Gas Mark 6 and grease the dish.

2. To prepare the pastry put the oats, flour, and salt in the bowl and mix; then add the butter and mix until you get a pebbly coarse texture.

3. Add the buttermilk and mix to combine.

4. Form the mixture into a ball and place it between 2 large pieces of cling film.

5. Roll out into a circle about 10 inches in diameter.

6. Remove the top sheet of cling film.

7. Transfer the pastry, still on the other piece of cling film to the pie dish; then remove the remaining portion of cling film.

8. Press the pastry gently into the dish.

9. Bake for 9 minutes, then let cool.

For the filling:

1. To prepare the filling, heat 2 teaspoons of oil in a large nonstick pan over a low heat.

2. Add the onion and cook, occasionally stirring, until golden brown and caramelized about 15 minutes.

3. Transfer the onions to a bowl.

4. Add the remaining 2 teaspoons of oil to the pan and heat over a medium-high heat.

5. Add the mushrooms, stirring occasionally, and cook until they begin to brown, about 6 minutes.

6. Add the onions back to the pan, stir in the salt, pepper, mustard, and thyme.

7. In a medium bowl whisk together the eggs, egg whites and evaporated milk.

8. Sprinkle the cheese into the pastry case.

9. Top with the mushroom-onion mixture and pour the egg mixture on top.

10. Reduce oven temperature to 180°C / 350°F / Gas Mark 4.

11. Bake for 40 minutes or until knife inserted in the middle comes out clean.

## Serving Suggestions

Serve with a light and a crispy side salad.

# CHEESE AND HAM BAGEL

Quick and Easy

Nothing beats a classic combination like ham and cheese, so why not give this ham and cheese bagel with a bit of a twist a go!

**Ingredients - Serves 1 Adult**

- ½ a wholemeal bagel

- 30g / 1oz. of low-fat cheese, grated

- 1 slice of ham

- 2 slices of tomato

- 4 slices of cucumber

- 2 lettuce leaves

## Method

1. Toast the bagel half and top with the ham, cheese, and salad vegetables.

## Serving Suggestions

Why not top your bagel with the ham and cheese, then place it under the grill until the cheese has melted!

## Info

Bagels are perfect for preparing a healthy snack in a flash.

## About this Recipe

A great recipe that the whole family will love!

# CHICKEN AND AVOCADO SALAD

This is easy to prepare and is versatile.

It can be a meal for the family or is just as useful if you're entertaining guests, and you need something quick yet nutritious.

## Ingredients - Serves 4 Adults

- 2 ripe avocados, peeled and stone removed

- 390g / 14 oz. of skinless and boneless chicken fillets, around 3 fillets

- 1 tablespoon of olive oil

- Chopped fresh parsley, as desired

- Freshly ground pepper, to taste

## Method

1. Cook the chicken under a grill or nonstick pan

2. While that's cooking, chop the avocados into small cubes

3. Mix the olive oil and pepper with a fork

4. Remove the chicken and cut into strips
5. Serve in a salad bowl with the avocado

6. Drizzle the oil on top and garnish with the parsley according to taste

## Serving Suggestions

Serve with some crusty brown bread or baby boiled potatoes.

# CHICKEN AND PASTA SALAD

A quick and easy lunch!

This is the perfect salad to make for a healthy lunch option that is packed with protein and low in fat and sugar.

## Ingredients - Serves 4 Adults

- 1 red pepper, thickly sliced.

- 1 red onion, thickly sliced.

- 10ml of olive oil.

- 300g of pasta.

- 4 chicken breasts.

- 2 garlic cloves, crushed.

- 150g of cherry tomatoes halved.

- 50g of salad leaves, such as rocket.

- 1 tablespoon of white wine vinegar.

## Method

1. Preheat the oven to 200°C / 400°F / Gas Mark 6.

2. Mix the pepper and onion with 1 tablespoon oil and roast for 20 minutes.

3. Cook the pasta according to packet instructions, drain and set aside.

4. Slice the chicken into bite-size pieces.

5. Heat the remaining oil in a frying pan over medium heat.

6. Fry the chicken for 6-8 minutes until cooked and no pink in the middle.

7. Mix the pasta, chicken, onion, pepper, cherry tomatoes, rocket, and vinegar in a bowl and serve.

# CHICKEN CAESAR SALAD

A quick and tasty lunch!

This delicious salad is quick to make and is excellent for a lunchtime meal. It is also great as a first course for a more formal dinner.

**Ingredients - Serves 4 Adults**

- 1 medium ciabatta loaf.

- 30ml of olive oil.

- 2 chicken breasts.

- 1 large cos lettuce.

- 6 tablespoons of Caesar dressing.

- Parmesan cheese for serving.

## Method

1. Preheat the oven to 200°C / 400°F / Gas Mark 6.

2. Slice the ciabatta with a bread knife into crouton sized pieces.

3. Spread the bread over a baking tray and sprinkle over 20ml of olive oil.

4. Bake for 8-10minutes, turning regularly until evenly brown.

5. Heat 10ml of olive oil in a frying pan over medium heat.

6. Place the chicken in the pan and fry for 4 minutes.

7. Turn the chicken and cook for a further 4 minutes.

8. Tear the lettuce into large pieces and place in a bowl.

9. Pull the chicken into bite-size strips and scatter over the lettuce, along with the croutons.

10. Drizzle the dressing over the salad and sprinkle with parmesan to serve.

# COUSCOUS SALAD

Suitable for vegetarians.
Are you looking for a tasty and nutritious summer lunch? This couscous salad is your answer and only takes 15 minutes to prepare. Why not add some chili, paprika, turmeric or cumin for a spicy alternative.

## Ingredients - Serves 1 Adult

- 60g / 2oz. of couscous.

- 2 tablespoons of chickpeas.

- 4 cherry tomatoes, halved.

- 1 small red pepper, finely sliced.

- 4 slices of cucumber, finely chopped.

- ½ garlic clove, crushed.

- ¼ lemon, juiced.

- Black pepper, to taste.

- ½ teaspoon of mixed herbs.

## Method

1. Tip the couscous into a medium-sized bowl and pour enough boiling water over to cover all of the couscous grains.

2. Cover and leave for 10 minutes or until all the water has been absorbed.

3. Fluff up the couscous with a fork before adding the remaining salad ingredients and mixing well.

## Serving Suggestions

Serve with a roast vegetable salad.

## Info

This a tasty twist on your standard salad and can be made the night before and kept in the fridge.

# CREAM OF MUSHROOM SOUP

This is a hearty and warming soup.

This is a hearty and warming soup that is very easy to make –
even if you have never cooked before.

### Ingredients - Serves 4 Adults

- 10 mushrooms, chopped.

- 1 medium onion, finely chopped.

- 2 cloves of garlic, finely chopped.

- 50g / 2 oz. of plain flour.

- 1 teaspoon vegetable oil.

- 425ml / ¾ pint of semi-skimmed milk.

- 575ml /1-pint stock (1 low salt vegetable stock cube dissolved in 575ml /1 pint of hot water).

- Salt and pepper to taste.

## Method

1. Heat the oil in a saucepan.

2. Add the mushrooms, onion and garlic and fry, stirring continually for 5 minutes.

3. Add the flour and stir well. Cook for another 2 minutes.

4. Gradually stir in the stock and milk and bring to the boil.

5. Keep stirring.

6. Simmer for 20 minutes, until thickened.

7. Add salt and pepper, to taste.

## Serving Suggestions

Serve with crusty wholemeal bread.

**Info**

Try using a variety of mushrooms or other vegetables such as celery. For flavor try thyme, parsley, or mixed herbs.

# FARMHOUSE VEG SOUP

3 of your 5 a day.

This wonderful soup will keep you warm and full and can be counted as one of your 5 a day!

## Ingredients - Serves 4 Adults

- 3 medium carrots.

- 1 medium turnip.

- 1 medium parsnip.

- 2 leeks.

- 1 medium onion.

- 8 mushrooms.

- 3 medium tomatoes.

- 1 teaspoon of vegetable oil.

- 50g / 2 oz. of plain flour.

- 150ml / ¼ pint of semi-skimmed milk.

- 2 vegetable stock cubes dissolved in 1 liter/ 1¾ pints of water.

- Salt and pepper to season.

## Method

1. Wash, peel and dice carrots, turnips and parsnips.

2. Wash and chop leeks, chop onion and sliced mushrooms.

3. Chop the tomatoes.

4. Heat the oil in a large saucepan, and gently fry onion and mushrooms.

5. Add carrots, turnips, parsnips, and leeks and fry gently.

6. Stir in the flour to absorb fat, gradually stir in the semi-skimmed milk.

7. Add stock and bring to boil, stirring continuously.

8. Add tomatoes, pepper and a pinch of salt if desired.

9. Cover saucepan and simmer gently for about 45 minutes.

## Serving Suggestions

Serve with crusty wholemeal bread.

# GREEK PASTA SALAD

A perfect summer lunch.

This salad is a real crowd-pleaser at a BBQ. It's so easy to make and is summer in a bowl. The perfect salad to pack and take to work too.

### Ingredients - Serves 4 Adults

- 250g of pasta.

- ½ cucumber.

- 200g of feta.

- 1 red onion.

- 125g of cherry tomatoes halved.

- 20ml of olive oil.

- 1 tablespoon of red wine vinegar.

- 2 teaspoons of dried oregano.

- Juice ½ lemon.

**Method**

1. Cook the pasta according to packet instructions.

2. Drain and cool under cold water.

3. In a small bowl, whisk together olive oil, red wine vinegar, lemon juice, and dried oregano.

4. Halve the cucumber and cut into thick slices.
5. Place the pasta, cucumber, red onion, tomatoes, crumbled feta cheese and dressing in a bowl and gently mix, then serve.

# GREEN CHICKEN SALAD

A lettuce-free salad!

Don't be put off by all the raw vegetables here – they go well together, and it is good to realize that not all salads have to be about tomatoes and lettuce.

**Ingredients - Serves 1 Adult**

- 1 breast of chicken, grilled and sliced or use any leftover chicken you might have from a roast.

- ⅓ of a head of broccoli.

- 2 sticks of celery.
- 2 spring onions or scallions.

- 1 green apple, preferable Granny Smith's.

- 1 teaspoon mixed fresh thyme and rosemary, well chopped.

- 1 dessertspoon of low-fat French dressing.

## Method

1. To mix this salad thoroughly, you will need a large bowl.

2. Add the cooked, sliced chicken to the bowl.

3. Break the broccoli into bite-size florets and add to the bowl with the sliced celery, chopped apple, and finely sliced spring onions or scallions.

4. Sprinkle over the fresh herbs and pour over 1 dessertspoon of the dressing.

## Serving Suggestions

Use this as a side salad if serving more than one person.

## Info
You can also top this salad with a mixture of seeds like pumpkin, sunflower seeds or pine nuts for extra crunch.

# GREEN PEA SOUP WITH BACON

An ideal starter or a tasty lunch.

This soup has lovely flavors through the combination of fresh mint and lean bacon.

### Ingredients - Serves 4 Adults

- 500g / 17½ oz. of frozen green peas, defrosted first.

- 2 tablespoons of olive oil.

- 2 garlic cloves.
- 1 medium onion.

- 1 liter of water.

- 2 tablespoons of chopped mint.

- 2 tablespoons of chopped parsley.

- 2 lean rashers, sliced thinly.

- 1 vegetable stock cube.

- Fresh ground black pepper, to taste.

## Method

1. Heat the oil in a saucepan over a medium heat.

2. Add the garlic and onion, cooking until they soften.

3. Stir to avoid them going brown and sticking to the pan.

4. Add the water, stock cube, peas, mint, and parsley.

5. Bring to the boil and then reduce the heat, cooking the mixture through for 8 minutes.

6. Remove from the heat and leave for a few minutes until the pan cools.

7. Get a food blender or processor and whiz the soup mix until smooth.

8. Trim the rashers of any fat and grill them until they go crispy and crumble up.

9. When the soup is ready, pour it into bowls and serve with the pepper and rashers on top.

**Serving Suggestions**

Serve with crusty wholemeal bread.

# GREGORY'S TORTILLA

Suitable for vegetarians

Eggs are a great choice to make a quick, easy, and nutritious lunch.

### Ingredients - Serves 4 Adults

- 1 large onion, finely chopped.

- 5 medium-size eggs.

- 1 red pepper, diced.

- 4 large whole grain pita bread.

- 1 teaspoon sunflower oil.

- Salt and pepper, to taste.

## Method

1. In a large frying pan fry the onion in a little sunflower oil until the onion starts to turn clear.

2. Beat the eggs and milk together and season with a little salt and pepper.

3. Pour in the eggs and using a spatula, mix the eggs around making sure they don't stick to the bottom of the pan.

4. Add in the diced red pepper.

5. Once you have mixed them in gently remove the pan from the heat and place under grill allowing the top to cook.

6. Once the top becomes solid and starts to brown under the grill remove it and cut into 4 portions.

7. Toast the pitta bread, then put one slice of the egg into each pitta and serve.

**Serving Suggestions**

You could also leave to cool and serve cold in a lunch box.

**Info**

Store any leftovers in your fridge

# GRILLED CHICKEN AND SALAD SANDWICH

Nutritious and delicious!

Quick and easy lunchbox filler suitable for the whole family.

## Ingredients - Serves 1 Adult

- 2 slices of wholegrain bread.

- 1 medium chicken breast fillet.

- 1 handful of salad leaves.

- 1 teaspoon of tomato relish.

## Method

1. Use a clean rolling pin to flatten the chicken. It will tenderize and cook faster.

2. Grill the chicken or cook it in a nonstick pan until cooked thoroughly, and all juices run clear.

3. Place the salad leaves on the bread and spread the tomato relish on the other slice.

4. When the chicken has cooled, place it in the sandwich.

5. Wrap the sandwich in greaseproof paper until it is ready to eat.

**Info**

To keep your lunches interesting, swap the tomato relish with a little honey & mustard or french dressing.

# GRILLED SALMON AND WARM NEW POTATO SALAD

A healthy delicious lunch.

A lot of people enjoy tuna at lunchtime, but why not try something different and opt for salmon? Served with baby potatoes and a colorful salad, this recipe is filling and will help keep your hunger at bay until dinner time!

**Ingredients - Serves 1 Adult**

For the salad:

- 4 medium new potatoes (160g / 5½oz.), quartered.

- 1 teaspoon of red or white wine vinegar.

- 1 salmon fillet (100g / 3½oz.).

- 30g / 1oz. of lettuce.

- 5 cherry tomatoes, halved.

- 6 slices of cucumber.

For the salad dressing:

- 1 tablespoon of low-fat natural yogurt.

- 1 teaspoon of reduced-fat mayonnaise.

- 1 scallion, sliced.

- Black pepper, to taste.

## Method

1. Preheat the grill to medium heat and line the grill pan with foil.

2. Grill the salmon fillet for 5-7 minutes on each side. You can allow it to cool or eat it warm.

3. Boil the new potatoes and when cooked, drain and immediately toss in the red or white wine vinegar.

4. Combine the yogurt, mayonnaise, scallion, and black pepper to make the potato salad dressing.

5. When the potatoes have cooled, slice into bite-sized chunks or pieces and then coat in the dressing.

6. Tomato, cucumber, and lettuce make a perfect basic salad to serve with the grilled salmon and potato salad.

**Serving Suggestions**

Serve with a lemon wedge.

**Info**

Any leftover new potatoes from dinner can be quickly reheated the next day and used in this tasty salad. No waste!

**About this Recipe**

You should aim to eat at least two portions of fish per week, and one of these portions should be an oily fish like salmon.

# HAM, CHEESE AND TOMATO TORTILLA

Ham, cheese, and tomato sambo with a twist!

Ham, cheese, and tomato sambos are an old favorite but can be a bit boring. Give them a new lease of life with this recipe.

## Ingredients - Serves 1 Adult

- 1 medium wholemeal flour tortilla/wrap.

- 1 dessertspoon of low-fat cream cheese.

- 2 slices of ham.

- 3 cherry tomatoes.

- 1 dessertspoon fresh basil leaves.

## Method

1. Lay the tortilla out flat on a cutting board and spread the cream cheese from edge to edge.

2. Lay the ham slices in the middle of the tortilla.

3. Next, chop the tomatoes into thin slices.

4. For that something extra, take a few of the fresh basil leaves and sprinkle them over the tomato.

5. Starting at the edge, roll the tortilla tightly until you have made a sausage shape. Cut into four pieces and pop into your lunchbox.

**Serving Suggestions**

You could also use slices of roast beef or turkey instead of ham; and cucumber or peppers instead of tomatoes.

**Info**

If you're making these the night before for your child's lunchbox, make sure you store it in your fridge until they're heading to school.

# HERB COUSCOUS

Suitable for vegetarians.

This middle eastern dish is a great addition to any BBQ.

### Ingredients - Serves 4 Adults

- 300g / 10½ oz. of couscous.

- 2 tablespoons of extra virgin olive oil.

- 1 small red onion, peeled.

- ½ red pepper, de-seeded.

- ½ yellow pepper, de-seeded.

- ½ courgette.

- 4 scallions, thinly sliced.

- Little bunch mint, chopped.

- Little bunch basil, chopped.

- Little bunch coriander, chopped.

- Freshly ground black pepper, to taste.

## Method

1. Cook the couscous according to the packet instructions, then set aside to cool.

2. Place half the olive oil in a frying pan over medium heat. Dice the onion and peppers and sauté in the oil.

3. Trim and slice the scallions and courgette and toss into the pan and then cook the vegetables for another couple of minutes until they start to brown, then remove from the heat and leave to cool.

4. Place the couscous in a large bowl and stir in the cooked vegetables.

5. Add the chopped herbs, some black pepper, and drizzle with the rest of the olive oil.

6. Mix thoroughly and keep chilled until ready to serve.

## Serving Suggestions

Couscous and be served cold as part of a salad or hot with your barbeque food.

# HOMEMADE TOMATO SALSA AND RYE CRISPBREAD

Suitable for vegetarians.

This lunch is quick and easy to prepare as well as being both tasty and nutritious. This recipe would make a perfect, refreshing lunch on a warm, summer day.

## Ingredients - Serves 1 Adult

- 2 medium tomatoes, finely chopped.

- 1 scallion, finely chopped.

- ½ tablespoon of fresh coriander, chopped.

- 1 teaspoon of olive oil.

- 1 pinch of cumin seeds.

- 1 pinch of crushed chili.

- ½ clove of garlic, peeled and crushed or finely chopped.

- ½ lime, juiced.

- 2 rye crispbreads.

## Method

1. Combine all of the ingredients in a bowl and mix gently.

2. Spread on the crispbread and enjoy.

3. Double or triple the ingredients for extra tomato salsa, which can be covered and refrigerated and used again.

## Serving Suggestions

Serve with a mixed leaf salad.

## Info

This salsa recipe would also be great alongside a barbeque. If you like your salsa with a kick, you can add a pinch more chili to make it as spicy as you like.

# HOMEMADE VEGETABLE SOUP

Suitable for vegetarians.

Vegetables are an essential part of a healthy diet but also taste fantastic, especially when made into soup. This soup is very easy to make – even if you have never cooked.

### Ingredients - Serves 3 Adults

- 1 medium onion.

- 1 leek.

- 2 medium-sized carrots.

- 2 sticks of celery.

- 1 small turnip.

- 1 clove of garlic.

- 1 tablespoon of fresh parsley and thyme. You can use dried, but fresh always gives a better flavor.

- 1 tablespoon of olive oil.

- 8g / ¼ oz. Margarine.

- 850ml / 1½ pints of vegetable stock.

## Method

1. Heat 1 tablespoon of olive oil and the margarine in a large saucepan.

2. Chop the onion, carrot, celery, leek, and turnip into small pieces, around 1cm cubes.

3. Sauté all the vegetables in the oil for 10 to 15 minutes over low heat, stirring occasionally.

4. Then add the chopped clove of garlic, 1 tablespoon of herbs and 1½ pints of vegetable stock.

5. Bring the soup to the boil and simmer for about 40 minutes.

6. Taste it to see if it needs extra salt or pepper.

7. You can eat the soup as it is or cook it for another 20 minutes and liquidize it to make a smooth soup.

8. Add some chopped fresh parsley and serve.

**Serving Suggestions**

Serve with wholemeal crusty bread.

**Info**

Vegetable soup can also be made with chicken stock for extra flavor.

# HOT PASTA SALAD

Low in salt!

A delicious hot pasta that is a perfect lunch for the whole family. Low in salt and ready to eat in 20 minutes!

## Ingredients - Serves 4 Adults

- 300g of pasta.

- 4 tablespoons of light mayonnaise.

- Juice of ½ a lemon.

- 200g can of tuna.

- 2 red peppers.

- 1 red onion.

- Large handful of rocket.

## Method

1. Cook pasta according to packet instructions.

2. Place the mayonnaise and lemon juice into a large bowl and mix.

3. Place the tuna into the same bowl and mix well.

4. Slice the peppers and onion thinly and add to the large bowl.

5. Drain the pasta and mix in with the mayonnaise mixture.

6. Serve with a handful of rocket.

# HUMMUS AND SALAD WRAP

Suitable for vegetarians

With something sweet for after...

**Ingredients - Serves 1 Adult**

For the wrap:

- 1 wholegrain wrap  (about 64g / 2 oz.).

- 1 heaped tablespoon of reduced-fat hummus.

- 1 salad serving of rocket leaves (15g / 1/2 oz.).

- 1 small carrot, grated.

- 1 small tomato, sliced.

- 1 scallion, sliced.

- 2 tablespoon soft low-fat cheddar cheese, grated.

- 1 tablespoon sweetcorn.

Something sweet for after:

- 1 pot of low-fat yogurt (125g / 4 ½ oz.)

- Mixed berries (140g / 5 oz.)

**Method**

1. Spread the hummus onto your wrap and top with the fresh salad ingredients and grated cheese for a simple, tasty lunch that's ready in minutes.

2. For a healthy, satisfying dessert, pour your yogurt over fresh mixed berries and enjoy!

**Info**

If you prefer your wrap toasted and oozing with melted cheese, place it under a sandwich toaster for 4 minutes until heated throughout and crispy at the edges.

# CHAPTER 4: CHICKEN & FOWLS

## FRIED CHICKEN

### Ingredients

- 1 broiler/fryer chicken, cut into 8 pieces.

- 2 cups low fat buttermilk.

- Vegetable shortening, for frying.

- 2 tablespoons Kosher salt.

- 2 tablespoons Hungarian paprika.

- 2 teaspoons garlic powder.

- 1 teaspoon cayenne pepper.

- Flour, for dredging.

**Yield:** 3 to 4

**Method**

1. Place chicken pieces into a plastic container and cover with buttermilk.

2. Cover and refrigerate for 12 to 24 hours.

3. Melt enough shortening (over low heat) to come 1/8-inch up the side of a 12-inch cast-iron skillet or heavy fry pan.

4. Once shortening liquefies raise temperature to 350° F., Do not allow the oil to go over 350° F.

5. Drain chicken in a colander.

6. Combine salt, paprika, garlic powder, and cayenne pepper. Liberally season chicken with this mixture.

7. Dredge chicken in flour and shake off excess.

8. Place chicken skin side down into the pan. Put thighs in the center, and breast and legs around the edge of the pan. The oil should come halfway up the pan.

9. Cook chicken until golden brown on each side, approximately 10 to 12 minutes per side. More importantly, the internal temperature should be right around 180°. (Be careful to monitor shortening temperature every few minutes).

10. Drain chicken on a rack over a sheet pan. Don¹t drain by setting chicken directly on paper towels or brown paper bags.

11. If you need to hold the chicken before serving, cover loosely with foil but avoid holding in a warm oven, especially if it's a gas oven.

# BROILED, BUTTERFLIED CHICKEN

## Ingredients

- 1 1/2 teaspoons black peppercorns.

- 4 garlic cloves, minced.

- 1/2 teaspoon kosher salt.

- 1 lemon, zested.

- Extra virgin olive oil.

- Onions, carrots, and celery cut into 3 to 4-inch pieces.

- 3 to 4-pound broiler/fryer chicken.

- Canola oil.

- 1 cup red wine.

- 8 ounces chicken stock.

- 2 to 3 sprigs thyme.

**Yield:** 4 to 6 servings

## Method

1. Position the oven rack 8 inches from the flame/coil and turn broiler to high.

2. Crack peppercorns with a mortar and pestle until coarsely ground. Add garlic and salt and work well.

3. Add lemon zest and work just until you can smell lemon.

4. Add just enough oil to form a paste.

5. Check out your refrigerator for onions, carrots, and celery that are a little past their prime. Cut vegetables into pieces and place in a deep roasting pan.

6. Place chicken on a plastic cutting board breast-side down. Using kitchen shears, cut ribs down one side of the backbone and then the other and remove.

7. Open chicken like a book and remove the keel bone separating the breast halves by slicing through the thin membrane covering it, then by placing two fingers underneath the bone and levering it out.

8. Turn chicken breast-side up and spread out like a butterfly by pressing down on the breast and pulling the legs towards you.

9. Loosen the skin at the neck and the edges of the thighs. Evenly distribute the garlic mixture under the skin, saving 2 teaspoons for the jus.

10. Drizzle the skin with oil and rub in, being sure to cover the bird evenly. Drizzle oil on the bone side of chicken as well.

11. Arrange bird in roasting pan, breast up, atop vegetables.

12. Place pan in the oven, be sure to leave the oven door ajar. Check the bird in 10 minutes.

13. If the skin is dark mahogany, hold the drumstick ends with paper towels and flip bone-side up. Cook 12 to 15 minutes or until the internal temperature reaches 165°. Juices must run clear.

14. Remove and place chicken into a deep bowl and cover loosely with foil.

15. Tilt the pan so that any fat will pool at the corner. Siphon this off with a bulb baster. (This fat is great in vinaigrettes).

16. Set the pan over 2 burners set on high. De-glaze pan with a few shots of red wine and scrape brown bits from the bottom using a carrot chunk held with tongs.

17. Add chicken stock, thyme, the remaining garlic paste, and reduce briefly to make a jus.

18. Strain out vegetables and discard.

19. Slice the chicken onto plates or serve in quarters. Sauce lightly with jus and serve.

# CHICKEN KIEV

## Ingredients

- 8 tablespoons (1 stick) unsalted butter, room temperature.

- 1 teaspoon dried parsley.

- 1 teaspoon dried tarragon.

- 4 boneless, skinless chicken breast halves.
- 1 teaspoon kosher salt, plus extra for seasoning chicken.

- 1/4 teaspoon freshly ground black pepper, plus extra for seasoning chicken.

- 2 large whole eggs, beaten with 1 teaspoon water.

- 2 cups Japanese bread crumbs (panko), plus 1/4 cup for filling.

- Vegetable oil, for frying.

**Yield:** 4 servings

**Method**

1. Combine butter, parsley, tarragon, 1 teaspoon salt, and 1/4 teaspoon black pepper in the bowl of a stand mixer.

2. Place mixture on plastic wrap or waxed paper and roll into a small log; place in the freezer.

3. Place chicken breasts, 1 at a time, between 2 pieces of plastic wrap.

4. Squirt chicken lightly with water and squirt the top of the plastic wrap as well.

5. Pound to no less than 1/8-inch thickness.

6. Season each piece of chicken with salt and pepper.

7. Lay 1 chicken breast on a new piece of plastic wrap and place 1/4 of the compound butter and 1 tablespoon bread crumbs in the center of each breast.

8. Using the plastic wrap to assist, fold in ends of breast and roll breast into a log, completely enclosing the butter; roll very tightly. Repeat with each breast.

9. Place chicken in the refrigerator for 2 hours or up to overnight.

10. Place egg and water mixture in 1 pie pan and 2 cups bread crumbs in a different pie pan.

11. Heat 1/2-inch of vegetable oil in a 12-inch sauté pan over medium-high heat until oil reaches 375 degrees F.

12. Dip each breast in the egg mixture and then roll in the bread crumbs.

13. Gently place each breast in oil, sealed-side down, and cook until golden brown, approximately 4 to 5 minutes on each side, until the internal temperature reaches 165 degrees F.

CPSIA information can be obtained
at www.ICGtesting.com
Printed in the USA
BVHW092052190421
605311BV00002B/76